MY JOURNEY OF UNLEARNING

UNLEARN THAT WHICH NO LONGER SERVES YOU, REFRAME YOUR NARRATIVE, AND STEP INTO YOUR POWER.

CAN BE USED IN COMPANION WITH THE BOOK
UNLEARNED:
HONOR YOUR STORY, RELEASE RESTRAINTS & EMBRACE YOUR POWER

DISCOVER YOURSELF THROUGH REFLECTION
AND RECLAIM YOUR NARRATIVE

THIS JOURNAL
BELONGS TO:

_____

THIS IS YOURS.
YOUR EXPERIENCE.
YOUR AWAKENING.
YOUR POWER.

MY JOURNEY OF UNLEARNING

DATE :   /   /

PAST	**FUTURE**
I'm grateful for :	*Things I hope in the future :*
○	○
○	○
○	○
○	○
○	○

REFLECTION ON TENET #1

Unlearn the guilt and embarrassment that may be entrenched in retelling your story. Start by taking a hard look at yourself - all of you. Assess the small moments and grand decisions that have woven the tapestry of your life.

TENET #1: UNLEARN BY RECOGNIZING YOUR STORY:
Recall a story about yourself. What is it?

_____

_____

_____

_____

_____

_____

_____

_____

_____

How do you feel recalling your story?

_____

_____

_____

_____

_____

_____

_____

_____

_____

_____

What do you need to unlearn from that story?

What brought you into that awareness?

What will remind you to unlearn?

PERSONAL REFLECTION:

PERSONAL REFLECTION:

MY JOURNEY OF UNLEARNING

DATE: /   /

PAST	FUTURE
I'm grateful for :	*Things I hope in the future :*
○	○
○	○
○	○
○	○
○	○

REFLECTION ON TENET #2

It may be lengthy and cathartic. Take your stories, history, and present situation and place them under a microscope. There's so much help available; embrace it where appropriate to develop a mindset that is laser-focused on healing and progressing.

TENET #2: UNLEARN BY DECONSTRUCTING YOUR STORY:
How do you self identify?

How do your relationships contribute to your sense of self?

What beliefs have had the greatest impact on your identity?

What primarily influences your identity?

How do you define self-awareness?

PERSONAL REFLECTION:

PERSONAL REFLECTION:

MY JOURNEY OF UNLEARNING

DATE :   /   /

PAST	FUTURE
I'm grateful for :	*Things I hope in the future :*
○	○
○	○
○	○
○	○
○	○

REFLECTION ON TENET #3

Closely examine how your mind works. Analyze your reactions, opinions, responses, and thoughts to understand their source. Take the crucial step of identifying the origins of your self-narrative and understand its impact on your life.

TENET #3: UNLEARN BY UNPACKING THE IMPACT:
How do the negative stories impact you?

_____

_____

_____

_____

_____

_____

_____

_____

_____

How do you define personal worth?

_____

_____

_____

_____

_____

_____

_____

_____

In what ways have your feeling of worth been challenged?

How do you dispel such challenges?

What reminds you that you are enough?

PERSONAL REFLECTION:

PERSONAL REFLECTION:

MY JOURNEY OF UNLEARNING

DATE :   /   /

PAST	FUTURE
I'm grateful for :	*Things I hope in the future :*
○	○
○	○
○	○
○	○
○	○

REFLECTION ON TENET #4

Honor yourself through the blessing and release the shame of your story. There are many ways to receive this release. Employ gratefulness! As you bless others, you bless yourself. As you honor others, you honor yourself. As you thank others, you thank yourself.

TENET #4: UNLEARN BY
HONORING YOURSELF THROUGH YOUR STORY:
When do you feel most grateful?

_____
_____
_____
_____
_____
_____
_____
_____
_____

What do you do in these moments?

_____
_____
_____
_____
_____
_____
_____
_____
_____

How can you enhance your gratefulness practice?

How do you acknowledge your ancestors?

In what ways do you honor yourself?

PERSONAL REFLECTION:

PERSONAL REFLECTION:

MY JOURNEY OF UNLEARNING

DATE: / /

PAST	FUTURE
I'm grateful for :	*Things I hope in the future :*
○	○
○	○
○	○
○	○
○	○

REFLECTION ON TENET #5

Standing in truth is being 100% authentic to how you desire to show up in this world. It is how you opt to present yourself in every facet of your being. That is truth, and truth is based on individual necessity and the need to represent that.

TENET #5: UNLEARN BY STANDING IN YOUR TRUTH:
How comfortable are you with yourself?

_____

_____

_____

_____

_____

_____

_____

_____

_____

_____

How do you comfortably display your authentic self?

_____

_____

_____

_____

_____

_____

_____

_____

_____

_____

What assisted you most in creating this safe space?

How can you continue to celebrate or create this in your life?

What customs or practices do you follow that warrant evaluation?

PERSONAL REFLECTION:

PERSONAL REFLECTION:

MY JOURNEY OF UNLEARNING

DATE :   /   /

PAST	FUTURE
I'm grateful for :	*Things I hope in the future :*
○	○
○	○
○	○
○	○
○	○

REFLECTION ON TENET #6

Unlearn the fairytale and face yourself in your current iteration. This is the point of clarity. It's important to be honest, not just with the negative impact but also with the positive. Note the amazing positives and allow yourself to feel their impact.

TENET #6: UNLEARN BY GETTING CLARITY:
What fairytale narratives in your life can you assess?

_____

_____

_____

_____

_____

_____

_____

How does fear impact your thoughts?

_____

_____

_____

_____

_____

_____

_____

What are your mechanisms for maintaining self-confidence?

_____

_____

_____

_____

_____

_____

_____

What are your positive affirmations?

_____

_____

_____

_____

_____

_____

_____

_____

What positive truths do you focus on that supersede limiting labels?

_____

_____

_____

_____

_____

_____

_____

_____

_____

_____

_____

_____

_____

_____

_____

_____

_____

PERSONAL REFLECTION:

PERSONAL REFLECTION:

MY JOURNEY OF UNLEARNING

DATE :   /   /

PAST	FUTURE
I'm grateful for :	*Things I hope in the future :*
○	○
○	○
○	○
○	○
○	○

REFLECTION ON TENET #7

Get on a mission of joy. Self-affirm. It's alright if you don't know what to tell yourself. Get support and have other people speak well into your life. Open yourself to new options, possibilities and variations that bring transformation.

TENET #7: UNLEARN BY RE-WORKING YOUR NARRATIVE:
What narratives can you restructure?

_____
_____
_____
_____
_____
_____
_____
_____
_____
_____
_____

Which old narratives no longer serve you?

_____
_____
_____
_____
_____
_____
_____
_____
_____
_____
_____

What urgency do you have around making changes?

What tools or practices can you use to create your new narrative?

With these changes, where do you expect to see the most improvement?

_____

_____

_____

_____

_____

_____

_____

_____

_____

_____

_____

_____

_____

_____

_____

_____

_____

_____

_____

PERSONAL REFLECTION:

PERSONAL REFLECTION:

MY JOURNEY OF UNLEARNING

DATE :   /   /

PAST	FUTURE
I'm grateful for :	*Things I hope in the future :*
○	○
○	○
○	○
○	○
○	○

REFLECTION ON TENET #8

Create a space where you harness the power of your voice to shape your future. Shed the cloak of silence. Engage perseverance and a commitment to growth to discover the voice that has always been there!

TENET #8: UNLEARN BY FINDING YOUR VOICE:
What is your message for a larger audience?

What impact do you desire to have?

How can you be more intentional about your message?

_____
_____
_____
_____
_____
_____
_____

How can you refine your speech and communication further?

_____
_____
_____
_____
_____
_____
_____
_____

How can you leverage your message, method and platform?

_____

_____

_____

_____

_____

_____

_____

_____

_____

_____

_____

_____

_____

_____

_____

_____

_____

_____

_____

_____

PERSONAL REFLECTION:

PERSONAL REFLECTION:

MY JOURNEY OF UNLEARNING

DATE: /   /

PAST	FUTURE
I'm grateful for :	*Things I hope in the future :*
○	○
○	○
○	○
○	○
○	○

REFLECTION ON TENET #9

Eliminate chaos from mental, emotional and spiritual spaces. Get granular and address the mess. Get clear so that you know exactly how to focus. To adequately shed chaos, purge spaces, people, and activities.

TENET #9: UNLEARN BY SHEDDING CHAOS:
What makes you unique?

_____
_____
_____
_____
_____
_____
_____
_____
_____
_____

How do you frame your unique aspects?

_____
_____
_____
_____
_____
_____
_____
_____
_____

What areas of your life can you assess to begin to "clean house"?

_____

_____

_____

_____

_____

_____

_____

What activities, spaces or people no longer serve you?

_____

_____

_____

_____

_____

_____

_____

_____

What are the practices that bring peace into your life?

PERSONAL REFLECTION:

PERSONAL REFLECTION:

MY JOURNEY OF UNLEARNING

DATE :   /   /

PAST	FUTURE
I'm grateful for :	*Things I hope in the future :*
○	○
○	○
○	○
○	○
○	○

REFLECTION ON TENET #10

Be the one to break generational curses in your family. Be the one to rid your mind of faulty thinking. Be the one to create a blueprint for the life that you long for. It's time. Roll your shoulders back and keep your neck held high. Unlearn and awaken.

TENET #10: UNLEARN AND AWAKEN:
What is your vision for your great future?

_____

_____

_____

_____

_____

_____

_____

_____

What are the components of your vision?

_____

_____

_____

_____

_____

_____

_____

_____

Who does your vision impact?

What new narrative do you need to embrace this vision?

In addition to unlearning, what new elements will you incorporate?

PERSONAL REFLECTION:

PERSONAL REFLECTION: